a rocky ROAD

a rocky ROAD

DEVOTIONS for losing weight

r. lynn frame

❊

Judson Press
Valley Forge

a rocky ROAD: DEVOTIONS for losing weight

Library of Congress Cataloging-in-Publication Data

Frame, R. Lynn.
    A rocky road : devotions for losing weight / R. Lynn Frame.
    p. cm.
ISBN 0-8170-1440-3 (pbk. : alk. paper)
    1. Weight loss—Religious aspects. 2. Motivation (Psychology) I. Title.

RM222.2 .R559 2003
613.2'5—dc21   2002073074
Printed in the U.S.A.

08 07 06 05 04 03 02
10 9 8 7 6 5 4 3 2 1

contents

❋ ❋ ❋ ❋ ❋ ❋ ❋ ❋ ❋ ❋ ❋ ❋ ❋ ❋ ❋ ❋ ❋

VI **introduction**

1 **part one:** Perspectives for Guiding the Journey

21 **part two:** Self-Understanding

41 **part three:** Self-Discipline

59 **part four:** Welcoming and Pursuing Support

75 **part five:** A Proactive Plan

95 **part six:** Doing Your Part

117 **conclusion**

introduction

❀ ❀ ❀ ❀ ❀ ❀ ❀ ❀ ❀ ❀ ❀ ❀ ❀ ❀ ❀ ❀ ❀

THERE is one secret and only one secret to losing weight, and the secret is this: There are no secrets. Despite what all the infomercials and advertisements say, there are no shortcuts, no magical pills, potions, or programs that can succeed over the long haul.

No major mysteries await human understanding. Medical science knows exactly why we gain or lose weight: If we take in more calories than we burn, we gain. If we burn more calories than we take in, we lose. The process by which we burn these calories is called metabolism. We speed up the body's metabolism by exercising. Thus, the more we exercise, the more we can eat without worrying about gaining weight. Simple enough?

Although the formula is simple, losing weight is hard, very hard—a long and rocky road. In fact, for many who have tried repeatedly, it seems impossible. Perhaps this is why so many people give in to one weight-loss scheme or another. Such schemes respond to the psychological need to believe that there is an easier way, something that will actually work and work quickly without pain or sacrifice. Unfortunately, simply believing something will work does not make it work, as many have learned the hard way and others have yet to learn and perhaps never will.

Unlike the promises made by many others, I can't guarantee that this book will produce the results you may be seeking. But I can guarantee that I will try to tell you the truth. And no weight-loss program can succeed if it is not rooted in truth.

The truth is that you may not be able to make it to the weight range where all those charts say you should be. And you may never be recruited as a fashion model. The truth, as attested to by the medical community, is that our ability to control our weight is to some extent limited. Certainly one good way to control our weight is to pick the right parents. Unfortunately, it's a bit late for that.

One important piece of truth, however, is that there are many things we *can* do to make our bodies—these temples of God's Holy Spirit—healthier. We can seek to better understand our eating habits. We can become more proactive in achieving weight- and health-related goals. We can adopt new perspectives and attitudes that increase motivation and the capacity for self-discipline.

Ultimately, the effort to lose weight and become healthier is not a physical struggle, but a spiritual one. Many of the principles and disciplines that lead to spiritual maturity correspond with those required to move toward victory in the area of physical health. Through daily devotional readings, we will explore these principles together and will do so from a variety of perspectives. Not everything will apply equally to all readers, because each person's struggles and sources of motivation are unique. I am confident, however, that you will encounter something new—perhaps many things—that will put you on a different path, a better path, one that will bring you closer to where you want to be. A path that, even if you fall short of your goals, will make you better off for trying. May God bless your journey as you, along with many others, seek to make this rocky road a bit smoother.

part one

PERSPECTIVES for guiding the journey

The first thing to fix
is our attitude.

GOD'S Surprises

❋ ❋ ❋ ❋ ❋ ❋ ❋ ❋ ❋ ❋ ❋ ❋ ❋ ❋ ❋ ❋ ❋

Now to him who by the power at work within us
is able to accomplish abundantly far more than all
we can ask or imagine, to him be glory in the church
and in Christ Jesus to all generations, forever and ever.
Amen. (Ephesians 3:20–21)

ONE of my many linguistic pet peeves is the overuse of
the word miracle. A miracle, by definition, is exceedingly
rare. Thus, if pretty much anything is a miracle, then
really nothing is.

I have an older friend, however, who likes to refer to
"God's surprises," a phrase I find more acceptable. God
can and does surprise us in pleasant ways. I'm sure we all
can point to situations in our own lives or in the lives of
people close to us that seemed impossible, irredeemable,
and beyond repair—for instance, a marriage that appears
to have totally broken down, a teenager on a path to
self-destruction, or a longstanding feud between siblings.
Then something happens. Something changes. Or *someone*

changes. And there is healing, restoration, hope. In short, God comes through with a little surprise. And the outcome is something we barely could have imagined.

This same dynamic applies to our striving to become healthier and happier, an effort that is ultimately a journey of faith. You may find it hard to imagine being able to jog or walk for three whole miles. You may wonder what it would feel like to be ten, twenty, thirty, or fifty pounds lighter. Or you may dream of hearing the doctor say to you at your yearly check-up, "I'm sorry, but you have absolutely no room left for improvement!"

We know how hard it is to lose weight and keep it off. But we also know it is possible. I suspect that most of us know at least a few people who made a decision, turned a corner, set out on a new path, and ended up at a place they could not have previously imagined. In fact, now they have trouble visualizing the way they used to be.

A perspective of faith imagines the possibilities. If you can't imagine the possibilities, you run the risk of limiting them. Be open to experiencing God's surprises. And enjoy them when they arrive.

❄ ❄ ❄

PRAYER: Dear God, may I understand more fully that you have no limits. Increase my openness to the surprises you may have in store for me, and increase my commitment to pursuing them.

JUDGE NOT Thyself

❄ ❄ ❄ ❄ ❄ ❄ ❄ ❄ ❄ ❄ ❄ ❄ ❄ ❄ ❄ ❄ ❄

But the LORD said to Samuel, "Do not look on his
appearance or on the height of his stature, because
I have rejected him; for the LORD does not see as
mortals see; they look on the outward appearance,
but the LORD looks on the heart."
(1 Samuel 16:7)

WHILE doing research in the library at graduate
school, I overheard a woman on a pay phone calling
about a high school English teaching job for which she
had applied. Confidently, she told the potential employer
about all the things she knew, how well she could teach,
and how hard she would work. From the sound of it, this
woman had no flaws at all. I thought she was one of the
most arrogant people I'd ever encountered.

Over the next few months, I got to know this woman
a little better. She had a lot of knowledge and talent but

suffered from low self-esteem. I realized I had mis-judged her. In fact, I came to understand that it was not the person on the other end of the telephone line whom she had been trying to convince of her talent and abil-ity; it was herself.

How quickly and instinctively (and wrongly) we judge other people based on an isolated conversation or on what part of town they come from or on how much they weigh. We judge—and society judges—without knowing anything about the struggles with which a person must contend: genetic challenges, emotional issues, financial difficulties. All of these and more can influence a person's capacity to control weight and strive for health.

Not only are we quick to judge others, but we also may be quick to judge ourselves when we look in the mirror or see a recent snapshot and imagine how others must be looking at us. The world needs more compas-sion for and less criticism of those who are struggling. We can begin by caring for, understanding, and respecting ourselves. Based on this self-respect, rooted in God's love, we can find the strength to strive toward the goal of becoming healthier and happier.

❄ ❄ ❄

PRAYER: Dear God, my Creator, when I look in the mirror, help me to see myself not as I fear others might see me, but as *you* see me.

LOVE Unlimited

❊ ❊ ❊ ❊ ❊ ❊ ❊ ❊ ❊ ❊ ❊ ❊ ❊ ❊ ❊ ❊ ❊

And when he comes home, he calls together his friends and neighbors, saying to them, "Rejoice with me, for I have found my sheep that was lost." (Luke 15:6)

THOSE who are fortunate enough to have come from a supportive family have from infancy associated displays of love and praise with accomplishments: baby's first word, baby's first step, a good report card, a goal scored in soccer. We are conditioned throughout our lives to base our sense of self-worth on what we achieve. Our culture strongly reinforces this value, defining success largely in terms of what we do for a living, how much money we make, and the places we have been.

The parable of the lost sheep establishes a fundamentally different value system, a radically different concept of how love—specifically God's love—works. Especially when we consider that most people associate efforts to lose weight not with success but with failure, understanding and embracing God's perspective is a vital place to begin.

Jesus' narrative suggests that ninety-nine out of one hundred sheep have made it safely home. One is caught in the brambles, alone in the cold of the night, desperate and afraid. The world is satisfied with ninety-nine out of one hundred. It's a high enough percentage to keep a sheep business profitable. As for the one who didn't make it, it was probably his fault anyway. He was stupid to get stuck and too weak to get free.

God, in contrast, is not interested in assigning blame. And God's love is not satisfied with ninety-nine out of one hundred. God has to have them all, and God is more than willing to venture out into the night no matter how cold or dark it might be. God's love is unconditional and unlimited. No matter how much you weigh, what you look like, or how many times you feel you've failed, God still loves you completely.

Losing weight with the goal of becoming healthier is an opportunity each of has to make a positive change in our lives. It is something we ought to do for a variety of reasons. But one thing that is *not* at stake is God's love, which remains unequalled and unsurpassed regardless of your accomplishments or failures in this or any area of your life.

✳ ✳ ✳

PRAYER: Lord, I know that you cannot love me any more than you already do. Help me to understand this fully and to view my efforts to become healthier and happier as an opportunity, not a prerequisite to experiencing your love.

A NEW Direction

So if anyone is in Christ, there is a new creation:
everything old has passed away; see, everything
has become new! (2 Corinthians 5:17)

FOR several years I've been looking, but I have never been able to find a better lead sentence to a book than the one chosen by M. Scott Peck in *The Road Less Traveled:* "Life is difficult." In these three words, the author establishes that he understands his readers totally. That is, he feels their pain.

Truly, life is difficult. Very difficult. Sometimes it seems overwhelming. We have so many responsibilities and so little time—and even less energy. Many, especially homemakers, feel as if their lives are dominated by other people's needs. Yet no one looks after them.

Sometimes we fail to appreciate that losing weight is by no means an easy or passive activity. It's one more time-consuming thing to add to an already overloaded schedule. It takes a lot of time to exercise and to shop for and prepare food carefully. Carrot sticks are simple enough, but it takes time to prepare satisfying, good-tasting, healthy meals on a consistent basis rather than settling for something quick and easy.

When we feel the stresses of life, one of our responses is to eat more than we should. We gain weight and lose energy, which makes it harder to find the strength to exercise and in turn leads to more stress and unwanted pounds. It's the proverbial "vicious cycle" in which we feel as if life is spinning out of control and we have no way to stop it. Our weight and our ability to control it may be indicators of just how fast life is spinning. When we are caught in this cycle, it seems as if the solutions are too numerous, complicated, and time-consuming. We think of everything that we would have to change for our lives to be different, and we are overwhelmed. We end up paralyzed, unable to do anything.

Perhaps it will help you, as it has helped me, not to think about the many things that would have to change, but about the *one fundamental thing* that would have to change: yourself. Christian faith teaches the concept of conversion, which can be applied to many areas beyond the decision to follow Christ. At conversion we take on new perspectives, new attitudes, and a new direction— just the things we need to succeed.

❋ ❋ ❋

PRAYER: Dear God, I want things to be different, but sometimes I feel powerless to change anything. Give me patience. Give me hope. Give me strength to be different, to make a change, to take control of my life, to move in a new direction.

The Drive to SUCCEED

❈ ❈ ❈ ❈ ❈ ❈ ❈ ❈ ❈ ❈ ❈ ❈ ❈ ❈ ❈ ❈ ❈

But this one thing I do: forgetting what lies behind
and straining forward to what lies ahead, I press on
toward the goal for the prize of the heavenly call
of God in Christ Jesus. (Philippians 3:13b–14)

I'M not a big follower of pro basketball, but I confess
to being (along with most of the rest of the world!) a
huge admirer of Michael Jordan. He is, in my opinion,
the consummate athlete, combining strength, quick-
ness, intelligence, skill, endurance, artistry, spontaneity, and, most important of all, determination.

Ironically, my appreciation for Michael Jordan as an
athlete increased most, not because of one of his many
great games, but because of one of his worst games. In
fact, it was the first game he played after coming out of
retirement for the first time in the middle of the season
in 1995.

Almost to a person, opponents and other commenta-
tors stated in pregame interviews that Michael Jordan

would pick up right where he had left off a year and a half earlier, without missing a proverbial beat. Some stopped just short of predicting that he would win the game single-handedly for his team. And what was their reasoning? They thought he could do it for no reason other than that he was Michael Jordan.

Well, the prognosticators were wrong. Not only did his team lose the game, but Jordan, especially when compared to what fans were used to, just plain stunk. Later in the year, his Chicago Bulls were eliminated early in the playoffs.

Simply "being Michael Jordan" was not enough. His first return to basketball in essence told the world that what made him Michael was not just his natural ability, but an incredible amount of dedication, drive, hard work, and practice, all of which, after his return, contributed to leading his team to three more championships.

We sell ourselves short when we think we can't do something because we just don't "have it," when we think we could never jog for a certain amount of time or succeed at a certain sport or physical activity. To claim we just don't have it can be a convenient way to let ourselves off the hook and keep from trying. The truth is no one "just has it"—not even Michael Jordan. And so before we conclude that it is impossible to lose weight, we need to ask ourselves how hard we have really tried.

✳ ✳ ✳

PRAYER: Lord, you came to earth to comfort the disturbed but also to disturb the comfortable. Sometimes it's hard to ask for the latter. But it's necessary. Give me the courage to want to be challenged and the determination to rise to the challenge.

What FRECKLES Are Good For

I praise you, for I am
fearfully and wonderfully made.
Wonderful are your works;
that I know very well.
—Psalm 139:14

I'VE had freckles since the time I first set foot in the sun. Freckles make children an easy target of ridicule, so over the years my opinion of them has varied, ranging roughly from severe dislike to intense hatred.

I remember in my younger days reading an article about where freckles come from. It explained that the function of freckles is to protect the body from the sun's harmful rays. Finding this out didn't necessarily make me like my freckles any better, but it helped me at least to understand them, come to terms with them, and perhaps even at some level to appreciate them. They were only trying to protect me.

The body, in so many different ways, represents God's amazing handiwork. For example, when we go without food for too long, the body, freckle-like, adjusts. Metabolism slows down, and the body becomes more efficient at burning calories. Fat stays with us longer than before. This biological reality explains, in a nutshell, why losing weight by "starving ourselves" cannot work. In fact, it is a very deceitful approach, providing the illusion of success while merely setting us up for ultimate failure. If simply going without food would work, losing weight would be much easier than it is. I for one would gladly trade a week or two of total fasting for a year or two of unbridled feasting.

If we are to succeed at losing weight, we must accept our bodies and the laws that govern them, as opposed to thinking that maybe God did not give quite enough thought to this issue of adjustable metabolism. Truly we are fearfully and wonderfully made.

❋ ❋ ❋

PRAYER: Thank you, God, for the wonder of creation, including the wonder of the human body. Grant me the wisdom to work with what you have given me.

The Quest for BALANCE

If you have found honey,
>   eat only enough for you,
>   or else, having too much,
>   you will vomit.
> —Proverbs 25:16

OFTEN a person's weaknesses are the "flip side" of his or her strengths. The leader who is a brainstormer, an idea person, a creative "outside-the-box" thinker, may struggle with managing the details required to put ideas into action. The methodical planner, who likes to organize and make lists, may have no room for spontaneity. The mother who cares the most about the welfare of her children runs the greatest risk of "spoiling them" by denying them opportunities to become independent.

The challenge to find balance in our lives in many ways lies at the core of successful Christian living. We want to be humble in representing our values to the world without being overrun by the world's competing values. We seek the right balance between forgiving other people and condoning their actions. We strive to be sensitive to the fact that millions of people around the world face hunger daily without being so overburdened with guilt that we cannot enjoy what we have.

This same quest for balance is ever-present in our efforts to lose weight and become healthy. We seek balance between enjoying the gifts of life—including foods that are rich in calories but oh-so-tasty—and recognizing that we do not live by bread pudding alone. We seek to find the right balance between accepting ourselves as we are, while at the same time challenging ourselves (and perhaps others within our spheres of influence) to become better. Between misguided vanity and appropriate concern for physical appearance. Between "just saying no" to unneeded food and trying to understand more about the psychological reasons we may eat more than we should.

On a more practical level, we seek the right balance between exercise and diet in our efforts to lose weight. And we seek an exercise program that is moderate enough to be sustainable—that is, "doable" on a consistent basis over the long haul—as opposed to the quick fix of a crash.

The scriptural call to moderation is in essence a call to live thoughtful, discerning lives, which is what we should expect from a thoughtful, discerning God.

⁂ ⁂ ⁂

PRAYER: Lord, I confess my lack of understanding and my need for wisdom. Help me to find the right middle ground and give me the confidence that you are with me.

part two

SELF-understanding

We may not always like ourselves,
but we need to know and
understand what makes
us who we are.

Do You REALLY Want to Be Healed?

❋ ❋ ❋ ❋ ❋ ❋ ❋ ❋ ❋ ❋ ❋ ❋ ❋ ❋ ❋ ❋ ❋

When Jesus saw him lying there and knew that
he had been there a long time, he said to him,
"Do you want to be made well?" (John 5:6)

THE story of the healing at the pool of Bethesda is
among the most revealing in all of Scripture. Jesus asks
the paralytic man, "Do you want to be healed?" For
most, the initial reaction is, "What a silly question!" But
upon further reflection, the implications of this query
are profound.

"Do you want to be healed?" is no mere rhetorical
question. The truth is that some people do not want to
be healed of whatever ails them, for they have grown
comfortable with the lifestyle associated with the illness.

For this paralytic, perhaps the prospect of actually
being healed was wrought with all kinds of potentially
negative consequences. No longer would he be able to
depend on others. He might have to go out and tend
sheep instead of hanging out at the pool day after day.

He might have to own up to his responsibilities to his family or pay off his debts.

Each one of us trying to shed unwanted pounds must ask ourselves this same question: Do I want to be "healed"? That is, how much do I really want what I think I ought to want? If I would lose thirty or forty pounds, might that create more problems than it solves? Might it confuse the role I have been expected to play in my family? Might I fear the thought of being physically attractive to my spouse again because it could lead to expectations of sexual intimacy that I may not be ready to fulfill?

Those who say they want to lose weight would do well to examine some of the psychological and emotional factors that may be working at cross-purposes with the stated goal. We think a lot about the benefits of losing weight. But what about the potential drawbacks? Are those extra pounds helping us run away from issues we ought to be facing? How much do we, deep down, truly want to be healed?

❀ ❀ ❀

PRAYER: Dear God, bringing to the surface issues and injuries and struggles can be a very painful process. I don't always know where various feelings, reactions, and behaviors come from. Open my heart, and give me the strength to face what I might find there.

OWNING Your Own Behavior

❀ ❀ ❀ ❀ ❀ ❀ ❀ ❀ ❀ ❀ ❀ ❀ ❀ ❀ ❀ ❀ ❀

I keep the LORD always before me:
> because he is at my right hand,
> I shall not be moved.
>> —Psalm 16:8

A FEW years ago while attending a conference, I crossed paths with a former coworker I hadn't seen in about five years. At the time of the conference, I was in the midst of a successful period of getting into shape. In fact, I had lost about ten pounds over the previous month or so and was feeling pretty good about myself.

However, the last time my former colleague had seen me I had been considerably lighter. From his vantage point, I had not lost ten pounds but had gained about twenty-five. Not being the most sensitive creature God ever created, he politely said hello, and then, almost instinctively, commented, "Looks like you've put on some weight." (Notice I identified him as a former coworker, not a friend!)

My positive feelings were dashed in an instant. I gave up. *Why bother?* I wondered. It didn't take me long to find those ten lost pounds (and a few more to go with them). I had allowed a short statement from a person I barely knew and didn't especially like to defeat me. Had this comment come from a friend, the effects might have been even worse.

In retrospect, this incident helped me to understand how important state of mind can be and how easily my state of mind can be influenced by the comments (including unsolicited ones) of others. Sticks and stones can break our bones, but names and offensive comments can sometimes hurt even worse. Often these negative statements come not from people like my coworker, but from our culture, from billboards and TV commercials that say, "You're overweight. You should be ashamed of yourself."

Some of us are capable of simply disregarding the insensitive comments of others, but for most this is far more easily said than done, because the roots of such sensitivities run deep. Hard as it can be, however, we must try. We must own our own behavior regardless of what others think. Like John Nash in the movie *A Beautiful Mind,* we must allow our minds and not just our emotions to control our behavior. This is not an easy battle to win, but it is one we must fight.

✳ ✳ ✳

PRAYER: Lord, give me the strength to resist the temptation to allow others to define who I am.

In SEARCH of Love

The LORD, your God, is in your midst,
   a warrior who gives victory;
      he will rejoice over you with gladness,
   he will renew you in his love;
      he will exult over you
      with loud singing....
                    —Zephaniah 3:17

ONE of the things that unites all human beings is the need for love. Some need more love, more attention and sacrifice, than others. We need it to differing degrees at various stages of our lives. We need different kinds of love, different expressions. But we all need love. Those who seem as if they don't are just pretending. And some of us are very good at pretending.

One of the great ironies of life—and it's a tragic irony—is that people who need love the most are in many cases the hardest ones to love. The toddler who is not getting enough attention will find ways to remedy that problem even if it means she has to drive her parents mad in the process. Then there's the teenager who's discovered, without even being aware of it, that he'd rather have his parents yelling at him than not saying anything at all. Being acknowledged as a troublemaker is better than being ignored. It's a search for love. We can go all the way to the crankiest of cranky old ladies in the cranky wing of the nursing home. She's cranky because she's still lonely after all these years.

For some, whether they realize it or not, overeating is a search for love. Many teenage girls (and boys too), deprived of acceptance, overeat as a response, which makes it even harder to find the acceptance their spirits crave. And the problem is not limited to teenagers. Some of the loneliest people in the world are married people who are part of a secure, stable family and go to church every Sunday. They eat in response to a general feeling of angst, discontent, and unhappiness that comes from feeling unloved.

We can either go on feeling the way we feel and going to bed each night with a pint of ice cream. Or we can talk to someone—a friend, a spouse, a counselor—who can help us fill the void in more appropriate and productive ways.

❋ ❋ ❋

PRAYER: Is there a shortage of love in my life, O God? Grant me the humility to ask for help, to seek and find the love I need.

UNCOVERING the Past

For God did not give us a spirit of cowardice,
but rather a spirit of power and of love
and of self-discipline. (2 Timothy 1:7)

I GREW up in the 1960s in a small coal-mining town where money was scarce. Because my father lost his job as a result of polio, our family of six had to spend some time on welfare until Dad could retrain for an office job. Household goods were rationed. We had strict limits on how much milk we could drink. If we bought a six-pack of "soda pop," it was clearly understood that each person could claim one and no more. For our family, "eating out" meant a rare trip to a new restaurant that at the time was taking the country by storm. It was called McDonald's. I have no recollection of ever eating at a sit-down restaurant or going on an actual far-away-from-home vacation.

I grew up experiencing frugality not as an option, but as a necessity. Not to "finish your plate" was close to being considered a mortal sin. Eating in front of other people was even closer. And those starving kids in China were never far from our minds. This part of my past is so deeply engrained that I doubt I will ever be able to outlive it totally, although I have made progress. Anyone who has known someone who grew up in the Depression era knows how psychologically difficult it can be for some people to waste anything, especially food.

I exhibit these same tendencies. In restaurants I instinctively (some might say obsessively) eat after my children, consuming food I neither need nor desire just to keep it from being wasted.

My own challenge is to understand emotionally what I already know in my mind, namely, that cleaning up after others does not actually prevent food from being wasted. It's just being wasted in a different place, and I'm hesitant to mention what that place might be!

I recognize that not everyone will be able to identify personally with this struggle, but I offer it as an example of the intense psychological forces that influence our attitudes and behavior, including our eating habits. It is important for each of us to become aware of the forces operating "behind the scenes" in our lives. Awareness alone will not solve the problem, but it's the only place to start.

❈ ❈ ❈

PRAYER: We are, in part, a product of our experiences. I thank you for all my experiences, good and bad, because in your divine plan they are an important part of my journey. But accepting our experiences does not mean we must live with all of their effects. Help me to understand myself more fully and to use that understanding to gain greater control of my life.

THANKS a Bunch, Puritans!

❀ ❀ ❀ ❀ ❀ ❀ ❀ ❀ ❀ ❀ ❀ ❀ ❀ ❀ ❀ ❀ ❀

Therefore do not let anyone condemn you in
matters of food and drink or of observing festivals,
new moons, or Sabbaths. These are only a shadow
of what is to come, but the substance belongs to Christ.
(Colossians 2:16–17)

TO SOME extent, personal values are determined by
family origin. And each particular family's values have in
turn been shaped partly by its culture's values. In the
United States, the Christian church (especially in some
conservative circles) still bears the marks of influences left
by the Puritans. Many of us who grew up in the culture
of conservative churches instinctively feel guilty about
enjoying some of the things in life that God intended for
us to enjoy—everything from pride in personal appearance to sex.

Elsewhere in this book, I state that personal appearance
should not be the number one reason for wanting to lose
weight and become healthy. But here I affirm that it

deserves to be on the list. Various segments of the church have, in the name of modesty, traditionally frowned upon such enhancements to personal appearance as jewelry and makeup, as well as certain hair or clothing styles. There are those within and outside the church who think that if music sounds good it must be the devil's. This same mentality leads to the conclusion that "church ladies" must look bad to be good.

It is one thing to be obsessed, dominated by concerns of personal appearance. Or to dress in ways intended only to be provocative. But it is quite another thing simply to care about the way we look. No one should hesitate to cite "personal appearance" as a reason for wanting, literally, to get into better shape.

Furthermore, what Puritanical forces did to nice clothes and jewelry was nothing compared to what they did to sex. Many in the church continue to struggle with the feeling that sex (or certain kinds of sex) is somehow wrong. The same is true of other forms of enjoyment that have, in some church circles, been considered too "worldly." The end result is that the morally acceptable, pleasurable options in life are wrongly distorted in favor of food, which somehow never fails to win the church's stamp of approval.

God gave us many avenues by which to explore and enjoy life. Of course, the Bible provides moral guidelines, but we owe it to ourselves to determine if the guidelines we have been conditioned to follow are in fact biblical or if they owe more to culture. Indeed, self-understanding must include an understanding of where our values came from and whether or not we should cling to them or leave them behind. The implications for losing weight and becoming healthier may be greater then you realize.

※ ※ ※

PRAYER: Reveal to me my "hang-ups," O Lord. Show me how distorted values may be keeping me from reaching my goals.

MYSTERIOUS Forces

For as the heavens are
> higher than the earth,
> so are my ways higher than your ways
> and my thoughts than your thoughts.
> —Isaiah 55:9

I LIVED the ultimate Spartan existence during my college years. I rarely bought anything I didn't absolutely need, even in those infrequent times when I had a little extra spending money. My frugality included avoiding the temptation of the ubiquitous vending machines around campus, machines that dispensed all manner of junk food, which to a college student is exquisite cuisine.

One spring day I cashed a paycheck for sixty dollars just before going to a gymnastics class. I returned to the locker room to discover that my money had been stolen. Not that I would sneeze at losing sixty dollars today, but at the time it was a particularly devastating and disorienting experience. What I remember most about the incident was what I did afterward. Instinctively, I scrounged up some loose change from my dorm room, marched straight to a vending machine, and ordered up a helping of the aforementioned cuisine. It was chocolate, as I recall.

At the time, I was confused by this somewhat involuntary reaction. Of all the times to buy a candy bar, why, instead of tightening my economic belt, did I make an impulse buy immediately after seeing my net worth so dramatically reduced? Only in retrospect can I understand what happened. Had I not lost the sixty dollars, I probably would not have purchased a candy bar, even though I would have been in a better financial position to buy one, or even two or three. Reacting as I did was my way of responding to the threat that my choice to buy an occasional candy bar could be taken away.

I strongly suspect that there are many people who must contend daily with this or a similar psychological dynamic. Remembering what it was like as a child to go to bed hungry is not a pleasant memory to have. Attempting to "erase the tapes" of such experiences is strong motivation for eating unhealthy foods at inappropriate times.

Eating, for some, can be a way of overcoming a time in life when the next good meal could not be taken for granted. Perhaps it's time to work on allowing the past to remain in the past.

❋ ❋ ❋

PRAYER: Dear God, the forces with which I must contend in this struggle are often both strong and mysterious. Give me patience to allow you to loosen their grip on my life.

Breakable Family RULES

✳ ✳ ✳ ✳ ✳ ✳ ✳ ✳ ✳ ✳ ✳ ✳ ✳ ✳ ✳ ✳ ✳

Let us therefore no longer pass judgment on one another, but resolve instead never to put a stumbling block or hindrance in the way of another. (Romans 14:13)

A FEW years after the fall of communism in Eastern Europe, a friend of mine, a regular jogger who once ran in a marathon, visited Russia for about a month. Upon his return, he was thrilled to tell others about everything he'd learned and about what the people there were going through. He'd had a wonderful time, with one exception. Apparently, running in public was considered socially unacceptable. So to avoid embarrassing his hosts, he gave up a big part of his exercise routine for the time he was in Russia.

At first glance, it would seem that these cultural rules about exercising in public do not apply to U.S. culture. After all, every day across the land men and women, young and old, can be found walking or jogging through neighborhoods or around running tracks. Yet there is a sense in which each individual family, while sharing some overlapping cultural values, is a culture unto itself, with its own unique set of rules. And in many U.S. families, wearing sweatpants in front of the neighbors may be socially unacceptable.

Family rules need not be stated in order to be in effect. If a particular behavior (such as exercising in public) is not modeled or encouraged in the home, the message communicated is that the activity, if not unacceptable, is at least unimportant. In fact, unspoken family rules are often the most powerful ones. Often the people who are sedentary—uncomfortable not just with exercise but with the very idea of exercise—are merely conforming to their family rules. Unfortunately, often the rules that apply for boys in this regard are different from the ones that apply to girls.

Those who follow Christ, however, believe in a God who is bigger than any set of family rules, no matter how strict or deeply enforced. We believe in a God who desires to do a new thing in our lives even if it means that sometimes we have to break the rules.

❈ ❈ ❈

PRAYER: Dear Lord, help me to understand when the humiliation I risk is real and when it is "imagined," merely a result of family rules from childhood that need no longer apply in my adult life.

self-DISCIPLINE

Often, a successful journey comes down to saying yes or saying no to the right things.

RESISTING Temptation

❋ ❋ ❋ ❋ ❋ ❋ ❋ ❋ ❋ ❋ ❋ ❋ ❋ ❋ ❋ ❋ ❋ ❋

Stay awake and pray that you may not come
into the time of trial; the spirit indeed is willing,
but the flesh is weak. (Matthew 26:41)

IN 1999, Pokemon cards were all the rage. A few years
earlier, Tickle Me Elmo was hot, and prior to that it was
Cabbage Patch Kids. And let's not forget Beanie Babies
and Trolls.

During the 1998 Christmas season, the country was
under assault from "Furby frenzy." Every kid age ten and
under—and a high percentage of kids eleven and older—
simply had to have one. Parents took out ads in newspa-
pers offering to pay up to four hundred dollars for a
Furby. (The retail price was about thirty dollars.) Some of
these youngsters led Mom and Dad to believe that their
very survival depended on acquiring one. I have a word
for such kids: *spoiled*.

But actually it's not the kids who are spoiled so much
as their parents. After all, the parents are the ones who do

not have the discipline to tolerate all the whining and shouting and crying that come when little Junior does not get his way.

It is a simple fact of life that we cannot have everything we want. Some people have learned this truth better than others, but we all should be reminded of it every now and then. As for those things we *can* have, not all of them are things we *should* have. Likewise, not all the things we desire to do are things we ought to do.

Discipline becomes necessary when our desires are at odds with the commitments we are striving to uphold. To put it another way, the need for discipline makes its entrance when what we *feel* like doing is different from what we know we should do and what our innermost being desires to do. After all, if we craved broccoli and brussel sprouts instead of chocolate cake and peanut butter pudding, discipline would not be necessary. That is why temptation is so hard to resist.

However, our commitment to keep on trying—to strive to win over temptation more times than we lose to it—is what in many ways defines our efforts to become spiritually mature followers of Christ. Counseling psychologists tell us that we cannot always control our feelings, but we can control our behavior. Such is the essence of discipline. Indeed, doing what is right instead of what we feel like doing is the mark of the mature human being.

❋ ❋ ❋

PRAYER: Lord Jesus, as the spirits of your apostles were weak some two thousand years ago, so our spirits are weak today. But they are stronger than they once were. And by your grace, they will be stronger yet tomorrow and in the days ahead. We strive with confidence toward maturity, knowing that the most important battle has already been won. Amen.

BEING CONTENT to Be Satisfied

Give us this day our daily bread. (Matthew 6:11)

SEVERAL years ago I had the opportunity to treat a husband-and-wife ministry team to lunch at an all-you-can-eat buffet. At the time, my custom at such venues was none other than to eat all I could eat, including dessert. Usually when I finished, I was not just full, but downright uncomfortable.

The couple I was treating was known for their frugal lifestyle, so I was eager to see how they would handle the temptation of an all-expense-paid smorgasbord. Each of them had a modest salad and a bowl of soup. The wife was going back for a drink when she asked her husband if he wanted anything more. He thought for a moment before answering, "No, I don't think so. I'm satisfied."

He was satisfied. He could have eaten more but chose not to because he was content. I was not content merely to be satisfied. Instead, I insisted on going beyond satisfaction.

I've thought about that man's words many times over the years in conjunction with Jesus teaching his disciples to pray, "Give us this day our daily bread." Unlike the proponents of the so-called prosperity gospel, Jesus didn't teach us to pray for everything we desired or felt we needed. Rather, he said to pray just for bread to provide strength for another day to do God's will.

It is not what we have that matters most, but how content we choose to be. We gain weight in part because, unlike my guests in the restaurant, we don't quit when we are satisfied. We do not distinguish, as Jesus did, between eating to meet a basic human need and eating for sport.

Or course, it is not evil to enjoy good food in abundance. But we should recognize that the ability to do so is a blessing, not a right we can demand from God or from anyone else. It's a blessing many in the world do not enjoy. And for those of us who are trying to lose weight, it's a blessing we would be wise to forego a little more often.

❊ ❊ ❊

PRAYER: Lord, we confess that we sometimes fail to enjoy your abundance wisely. We have allowed it to shield us from the joy that comes from being content in simplicity. We take our wealth for granted. Give us the bread we need this day and every day. Satisfy us, O Lord, and then give us the maturity to be content with what you have provided. Amen.

Seeing Your Body as a TEMPLE

Or do you not know that your body is a temple
of the Holy Spirit within you, which you have from God,
and that you are not your own? For you were bought
with a price; therefore glorify God in your body.
(1 Corinthians 6:19-20)

THE most common reason people want to lose weight
is appearance. What ought to be the most common reason is health. This especially ought to be the case for
those who take the teachings of Scripture seriously.

Christianity is sometimes portrayed as a strictly spiritual
religion in which the "flesh" is regarded as evil, or at least
not as important as the spirit. Various groups throughout
history have emphasized the pietistic, personal holiness
(that is, spiritual) aspects of the faith while ignoring the
physical and social dimensions of Christianity.

The truth is that we are spiritual, social, *and* physical
beings. And Christian teaching has implications for all
these dimensions. God formed a material world; gave

humans physical bodies that are home to the divine, the Holy Spirit; and even came to earth in the form of a human body. Furthermore, traditional Christian doctrine upholds the belief in a future bodily resurrection. Nevertheless, it is a rare pastor who preaches about the importance of maintaining healthy bodies.

We preach, as we should, to our children and youth about the dangers of drug and alcohol abuse, but when it comes to a more complete concern for healthy bodies, not only is the church silent for the most part, but we supply the donuts and chips! (Keep in mind that in the United States each year an estimated three hundred thousand deaths are associated with obesity, while an estimated four hundred thousand are related to cigarette smoking.)

It is with our bodies that we carry out the work of the kingdom. We use our bodies to help build houses for those who can't afford them and to deliver meals to the hungry to demonstrate Christ's love for the whole person. Our bodies are the temples of the Holy Spirit. Let us not ignore the responsibility we have to care for them.

❊ ❊ ❊

PRAYER: Lord God, I confess that I have not always treated my body with the respect it deserves as a temple of your Holy Spirit. Give me strength to meet the challenge of treating my body with greater care.

CONTROLLING Your Environment

And if your eye causes you to stumble, tear it out;
it is better for you to enter the kingdom of God
with one eye than to have two eyes
and to be thrown into hell.... (Mark 9:47)

WHO has more discipline: the person who at 10:00 P.M. resists the calorie-laden peanut butter ice cream in the kitchen freezer or the one who, earlier in the day, decided not to bring the ice cream home?

Before answering the question, consider the difference in meaning between discipline and willpower. Willpower suggests the strength of will in a given moment to resist, to "just say no" to an opportunity that is right under your nose, perhaps literally. Discipline is a far broader, more inclusive concept. It includes, for example, the capacity to prevent that thing, whatever it is, from getting under your nose in the first place.

Discipline implies a strong element of self-awareness and common sense. That is, if we know at 3:00 P.M. that we're going to be tempted by ice cream at 10:00 P.M., the time to address the challenge is at 3:00, not 10:00. This constitutes a recognition of our weaknesses and struggles and the commitment to take greater control of our environment for our own good.

Plucking out the eye that causes us to sin can be viewed as instruction to steer clear of those things in life that we know from experience are likely to cause us to fall. A woman who struggles with alcoholism may not have the willpower to resist a drink when one is offered to her, but she can have the discipline to avoid venues where alcohol is likely to be present. A man who struggles with compulsive gambling can choose to vacation in Los Angeles instead of Las Vegas.

Each time we enter a grocery store, we have an opportunity to control our home environment, to limit the temptations to which we will be exposed. This does not mean that you should never enjoy ice cream at 10:00 P.M. or even at 10:00 A.M. if that's your style and preference! But as with all good things, it is to be enjoyed in moderation so it will not be a detriment to your health.

❉ ❉ ❉

PRAYER: I pray, dear God, for wisdom to anticipate my weaknesses and to address them in time.

Practicing DENIAL

Then Jesus told his disciples, "If any want to become my followers, let them deny themselves and take up their cross and follow me. For those who want to save their life will lose it, and those who lose their life for my sake will find it. For what will it profit them if they gain the whole world but forfeit their life? Or what will they give in return for their life?

"For the Son of Man is to come with his angels in the glory of his Father, and then he will repay everyone for that has been done." (Matthew 16:24-27)

MYSTERY and paradox consistently weave in and out of Christian faith and Jesus' teachings. Followers become true leaders. The first end up being last. The meek inherit the earth. The humble are exalted. An infant child is proclaimed king. What appears on the surface often points subtly toward a deeper meaning within, a hidden understanding longing to be brought to light. I see paradox at work in Jesus' admonition in Matthew 16 to deny ourselves.

Christian faith supposedly includes a healthy dose of happiness and joy. And the quest for happiness implies pursuing our needs and desires, going for the gusto, getting what we want and always wanting more. So what's this talk about denying ourselves? How is that supposed to give us joy?

Jesus understood far more than any of us what we truly need. After all, the evidence from human nature points to the conclusion that those who get everything they want end up wanting more, while those who have learned to deny themselves are more likely to cherish what they have and, consequently, find joy.

I am reminded of a scene from the movie *Chocolat*, in which a small French town's political leader is convinced it is sinful to eat chocolate and so denies himself—but not forever. When he does at long last experience the joy of chocolate, a more exuberant encounter is barely imaginable.

Likewise, the best hamburger I ever had was one I ate after going for more than a year without eating a hamburger. The "moral" of these stories is this: Paradoxically, if we want to increase our capacity to enjoy the good things in life, including the good foods, having the discipline to deny ourselves might be a good place to start.

※ ※ ※

PRAYER: Lord, thank you for not giving me everything I have ever craved or felt I needed. For otherwise, I wonder if I would be able to truly enjoy what I already have.

PLAYING by the Rules

For he makes his sun rise on the evil and
on the good, and sends rain on the righteous
and on the unrighteous. (Matthew 5:45b)

ONE of my three daughters loves athletics and is
involved in five different sports throughout the year. The
one where she stands to improve the most, however, is basketball. To help her improve her skills, I bought her a book
that was recommended by a women's basketball coach.

In looking over the book, I came across a very helpful
piece of advice that applies not just to basketball, but to
many areas of life. In fact, the author changed my perspective on the old adage "Practice makes perfect" by
stating, in essence, that it doesn't matter how *much* you
practice, but rather how *right* you practice. That is, unless
you practice the right things in the right ways, you get to
be very good at doing something wrong.

The implications for losing weight and becoming
healthier are clear. It doesn't matter how much we suffer

and sacrifice, how out of breath we get, or how much we sweat. The more closely we follow the rules, the greater will be our chances of achieving our weight-related and health-related goals.

I detect among some in the believing community a kind of subtle spiritual arrogance, one that tacitly presumes that the rules applying to "God's chosen" are somehow different from the laws that apply to others. We fail to appreciate that, by and large, the world God created functions based on cause and effect.

To have faith in God and to fulfill human responsibility are not mutually exclusive concepts. We may trust that God protects us, but we should still wear seat belts and look both ways before crossing the street. And if we eat too much of the wrong kinds of food while finding it easy to just say no to exercise, we will gain weight. And starvation-type diets are bound, by the laws of God's nature, to make things worse instead of better. These are the rules.

Some overweight and physically unhealthy people of faith are content to say, "This is the way God made me. This is who I am." But God also made us with the capacity to choose. And outcomes in this cause-and-effect universe—whether related to health and weight or anything else—will be influenced in large part by what we choose to do and not to do.

※ ※ ※

PRAYER: Dear God, protect me from the pride that subtly enters my life and influences my perspectives. Help me to accept that the laws of your universe apply to me as much as they do to anyone.

Setting a GOOD EXAMPLE

❋ ❋ ❋ ❋ ❋ ❋ ❋ ❋ ❋ ❋ ❋ ❋ ❋ ❋ ❋ ❋ ❋

Be imitators of me, as I am of Christ.
(1 Corinthians 11:1)

A FEW years ago, I had a chance to interview for a magazine story a very interesting woman who had suffered the misfortune of losing her right hand in a farming accident at age fourteen. Eventually Mary recovered from the emotional and physical trauma and learned to live with one hand. She did far more than merely "make do" or "get by." She thrived. She got married, had children, enjoyed a meaningful career in public service, and even wrote a book, typing it herself one-handed.

But the most interesting story Mary tells about being one-handed revolves around cooking. She had learned to do everything she needed to do in the kitchen with one hand—including cracking eggs. One day she decided it was time for her young daughter to help her bake a cake. After years of watching her mother, it was finally the little girl's turn to get her tiny hands into the mix.

Mary gave her daughter an egg and told her to break it into the mixing bowl. The girl took the egg and, without so much as a pause, executed the plan to perfection. And she did it with one hand just like her mother! Mary realized at that moment how closely her daughter had been watching her every move, mostly for good, but sometimes not.

According to researchers at the Centers for Disease Control, the number of overweight children has tripled over the last twenty years. Obesity-related illnesses, including diabetes, once thought to be confined to the adult population, are on the rise. According to a 1999 CDC study, more than one in eight children and adolescents in America are overweight.

Let us all (especially parents) remember that others—including those we love the most in this world—are watching. They are watching how and what we eat. They are watching if and how we exercise. They are watching, and they are learning. What are we teaching them?

※　※　※

PRAYER: Dear Lord, I desire to be a better example to all but especially to those who are younger than I. Help me to understand more fully that my responsibilities as a role model are important ones.

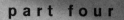
part four

welcoming and pursuing SUPPORT

Even the so-called
Lone Ranger had Tonto.
Ask for help.

Don't Go It ALONE

✳ ✳ ✳ ✳ ✳ ✳ ✳ ✳ ✳ ✳ ✳ ✳ ✳ ✳ ✳ ✳ ✳

> Two are better than one, because they have a
> good reward for their toil. For if they fall, one will
> lift up the other; but woe to one who is alone
> and falls and does not have another to help.
> (Ecclesiastes 4:9–10)

WE live in a culture that values independence, but we follow a faith that teaches that we have been created to live in community. When our rehabilitation system wants to punish someone who is already in prison, the person gets solitary confinement, which functions as a sort of prison within a prison. To be isolated from other human beings is its own, deeper form of punishment.

Yes, there are times when we crave privacy and solitude, especially if we spend our days with screaming, slobbering toddlers who seem to keep their diapers ever filled. But ultimately we were created to be a part of the larger human fabric. We need others, and others need us.

When I think about the most important lesson I can

teach my teenage daughters, one thing jumps to the top of the list: Do your best to look after yourself, but when you need help, ask for it. Ask your parents, teachers, friends, pastor, or coach. Ask someone who can help or can find someone who can.

I hope that other parents are teaching this lesson and also that we are "practicing what we preach." Losing weight and becoming healthier can in many ways be a daunting challenge both physically and spiritually. No person should have to (or want to) face it alone.

Striving with others toward the same goals provides a sense of commitment, responsibility, and accountability. It's hard to get up at 6:00 A.M. to go walking. But it's harder still not to show up if you know a friend is waiting to walk with you. There are many opportunities to build relationships while becoming healthier. Find a tennis or jogging partner. Form a support group to exchange healthy recipes, motivational tips, and encouragement. Take turns babysitting the aforementioned slobbering toddlers so everyone gets a chance to exercise. Turn your challenge into an opportunity.

❄ ❄ ❄

PRAYER: Dear God, I am not strong enough to win life's battles—including a battle with weight—alone. Help me to lay claim to your support and to the support of those you have placed in my life.

On RESISTING Chocolate

❋ ❋ ❋ ❋ ❋ ❋ ❋ ❋ ❋ ❋ ❋ ❋ ❋ ❋ ❋ ❋ ❋

When you make a vow to God, do not delay fulfilling it; for he has no pleasure in fools. Fulfill what you vow. (Ecclesiastes 5:4)

LIKE many other Christians around the world, before the beginning of each Lenten season I consider what sacrifice I might make to identify in some symbolic way with the sacrifice Jesus made on the cross. Not having been reared in a strict liturgical environment, this Lenten tradition is not as deeply engrained in me as I sometimes wish it were. Some years I don't give up anything for Lent. Other years I try and fail. When I am faithful in the endeavor, however, it is rewarding in a multitude of ways. For those who are trying to become healthier, giving up a favorite food during Lent is an opportunity to begin a new habit.

One year my teenage daughter, totally unprompted, announced that she and a friend had decided to give up chocolate for Lent. For some, giving up chocolate would not be a major sacrifice. For my daughter, it's the equivalent of Tiger Woods giving up golf. Because she plays several different sports, she's in top physical shape, which belies the fact that her diet revolves around the big C.

Wanting to support her effort, I decided to join her in giving up chocolate, which would be no easy task for me either. I made it through Ash Wednesday (in other words, one day!) with my resolve uncompromised. But the next day was Valentine's Day, and some generous soul decided to bring in to my workplace some homemade, heart-shaped chocolate cupcakes.

The process of rationalization and justification kicked in. "She'll feel bad if no one eats her cupcakes after all the trouble she went through to bake them." "I'll go ahead and eat it, then do some extra sit-ups." Before giving myself time to respond to these thoughts, I consumed the heart-shaped delicacy. Having gone without chocolate for nearly two days, I savored each crumb.

As soon as I finished it, however, I began to feel guilty. I realized that, yes, I could do some extra sit-ups to make up for the extra calories. But that wasn't the point. I had made a commitment to be in solidarity with my daughter, and I failed in less than two days. Among other things, I felt like a spineless wimp.

I determined to reestablish my commitment with new resolve. I reminded myself that this commitment was not just about me. And I was also reminded that being accountable to people we care about can be a strong motivator.

❋   ❋   ❋

PRAYER: Dear God, in those times when I am too weak to do what I should in order to improve myself, remind me that I am striving not just for myself, but for others whom I care about and who may be counting on me.

LIVING Water

Jesus said to her, "Everyone who drinks of this water will be thirsty again, but those who drink of the water that I will give them will never be thirsty. The water that I will give will become in them a spring of water gushing up to eternal life" (John 4:13–14)

RECENTLY, a coworker sent around an e-mail message announcing that she had brought in some refreshments to share. Someone asked if she'd brought something healthy. Making use of a telling euphemism, she replied, "No. I brought comfort food." In this particular case, the "comfort food" was coffee cake and donuts.

In more than one TV sitcom, we have witnessed someone (always a female) finding solace in a pint of ice cream or a box of jelly-filled donuts. Why is it that we find such foods comforting?

Some psychologists attribute it to conditioning. The argument goes something like this: When you were a little kid and you fell and scraped your knee, your mom, loving mother that she was, gave you candy to comfort you—and you've been going back to it ever since.

Far fewer people would be overweight if we ate only when hungry. The truth is that often we eat when we are not hungry. We eat because we're under stress or because we're anxious about something. Or depressed. Or lonely. Or bored. Perhaps all of the above.

In short, we eat because for some reason we feel bad. Instinctively, we look for a way to feel good—and the sooner the better. Food does the trick, but of course it has to be carrot cake and not carrot sticks. Unfortunately, food accomplishes its goal, not by addressing the source of the problem, but by covering it up, by helping us forget about our cares at least for a little while.

Just as anything short of living water cannot ultimately quench our deepest spiritual thirst, food cannot ultimately address the root of our troubles. The sooner we understand this, the further along we will be toward the goal of becoming healthier and happier. The next time you find yourself eating even when you're not hungry, ask yourself why. Consider a better way to address your problem. Use a lifeline: phone a friend.

※　※　※

PRAYER: Dear Lord, we seek comfort. The way is sometimes hard, and we need comfort. Help me to pause in the search, however, so that I can be sure to look for it in the right places.

It's a FAMILY Affair

Bear one another's burdens, and in this way
you will fulfill the law of Christ. (Galatians 6:2)

PSYCHOLOGISTS have noticed an interesting
dynamic that takes place when a spouse decides on his
or her own to get serious about losing weight and getting into shape. What often happens is that as one of
the two makes progress in losing weight, the other
starts to gain, almost as if there is some unwritten rule
that the couple's total weight must remain the same.
(This is more likely to happen if it is the husband who
decides to lose weight, given society's judgment that it
is more acceptable for men than it is for women to be
overweight.)

The most likely explanation is that the one "left behind"
in the weight loss initiative feels threatened by a sort of
implied expectation: "If my spouse has decided to lose
weight, that must mean he expects me to lose weight too.
But no one consulted me about this. No one asked if I was

ready or if I wanted to do this." And so, subconsciously, we assert our independence: "If he's going to lose weight, then I'll show him. I'll just go ahead and gain some."

In addition, again subconsciously, the left-behind spouse might try to subvert the weight-loss plan: "Let's see how good he is at resisting the smell of freshly baked chocolate chip cookies after his evening jog." And of course, if his willpower is stronger than she thought, guess who ends up eating the cookies?

Husbands and wives need as much support from each other as possible in all areas of their lives. They should talk about health-related goals and commitments—as they should talk about all things—especially if one or the other has a physical condition that places limits on diet or requires new commitments to exercise. It's unfair and insensitive to bring into the home environment items that will merely serve to tempt someone you are supposed to care about.

Families constitute one of life's strongest support systems—but only if we discuss goals and work as a team to help those we love most to achieve their goals, even if they are not our own.

❈ ❈ ❈

PRAYER: Thank you, God, for my family members. I need their support more than I sometimes realize. Open our eyes to ways we can support each other and to what we can accomplish when we work together.

When FRIENDS Are Not Enough

※ ※ ※ ※ ※ ※ ※ ※ ※ ※ ※ ※ ※ ※ ※ ※ ※

Without counsel, plans go
        wrong,
    but with many advisors,
        they succeed.
            —Proverbs 15:22

THE goal of becoming healthy should take precedence over the goal of reaching and maintaining a particular weight. True, there is a correlation between weight and health, but this correlation is not absolute. That is, there are plenty of "normal weight" people who are not as healthy as overweight people whose hearts and lungs are strong and whose cholesterol levels are normal. Those with eating disorders such as bulimia and anorexia may look fine on the weight charts, but no one considers them healthy.

Sometimes in our efforts to control weight and become healthy, we need more help than can be provided by a support group or relationship of accountability. We may need more help than our family and friends can provide. As we explored in an earlier devotion, some of the reasons we are unable to develop healthy eating and exercise habits have deep psychological and emotional roots. Women who have been sexually abused, for example, are among those who have a vested interest in gaining weight. Looking undesirable minimizes the risk of being expected to perform sexually. Perhaps exercise in your family of origin was a role claimed by someone else, and to try to occupy another's territory was considered inappropriate.

Some may have psychological aversions to exercise. This is especially true for men whose earliest associations include experiences of failure and embarrassment. I remember one particularly unathletic boy from grade school who became a target of intense ridicule every time he put on shorts and sneakers for gym class. Given what he had to endure, it would be hard to fault him for giving up exercise for life.

There remains today in some segments of the Christian community and in society a stigma associated with professional counseling. It's a sign of weakness or lack of spiritual maturity. Some people who visit their family physician for the smallest of reasons would never consider seeing a professional counselor.

Many of us know how possible it is to be lonely in a crowd—or in a family. We owe it to ourselves to explore all that might be keeping us from becoming healthier and happier. That includes being open to seeking professional help.

❋ ❋ ❋

PRAYER: Lord and Comforter, I seek humility. Help me to put concerns for my health above concerns for my image.

With a Little Help from a FRIEND

❋ ❋ ❋ ❋ ❋ ❋ ❋ ❋ ❋ ❋ ❋ ❋ ❋ ❋ ❋ ❋ ❋

Some friends play at
   friendship
 but a true friend sticks
   closer than one's
   nearest kin.
      —Proverbs 18:24

AS with most marriages, through the years mine has had
its ups and downs, its good times and bad. One of our
toughest times came after moving to a new area of the
country. Problems began to arise even though we had
already had three children together and had been through
all of the major adjustments young children require of a
marriage. Life was getting a lot more stressful for both of
us, and our marriage was being tested.

Through some counseling and a lot of thinking, however, we realized that something *had* changed—something very important. With our move, we had, in one fell
swoop, lost virtually all of our friends, mainly the four or

five couples from our church whose families had literally grown up together with ours. They were still accessible by phone or letter (this was before e-mail), but it wasn't the same.

We have many potential support systems: immediate family, extended family, neighborhood, community, church. Of all of them, I believe the most underrated is friends. Single persons need friends for both practical and emotional support. As for husbands and wives, it is unfair and unrealistic to think that one person can fulfill all needs, desires, and expectations.

Friendships are made, not born. They are created through acts of will, through taking risks and making commitments of time and energy. A few years ago, I took a risk at my daughter's softball game upon hearing that one of the softball parents was looking for a racquetball partner. I volunteered for the job. For most of the last three years, we've played at least two or three times a month. Our conversations are no longer limited to soft-ball and children; now they include social and religious questions. We are friends.

I have not seen any studies on the topic, but I would not be the least bit surprised to find a correlation between a shortage of friends and struggling with obesity. A friend can support us in many ways in our efforts to lose weight and become healthier. Not only can a friend be a walking or racquetball partner, but she can also be someone who listens and helps you respond in positive ways to the challenges you face.

Among God's greatest gifts to us are friends. Do you have a friend in your life? Do you have enough friends? If not, perhaps the time has come to take a risk or two.

❈　❈　❈

PRAYER: Dear God, as David had Jonathan and Naomi had Ruth, I desire to be rich with friends. Give me the courage to take the necessary risks.

a PROACTIVE plan

Think positive!
Not only is it biblical,
but it works!

PROACTIVE Faith

❀ ❀ ❀ ❀ ❀ ❀ ❀ ❀ ❀ ❀ ❀ ❀ ❀ ❀ ❀ ❀ ❀

But those who look into the perfect law,
the law of liberty, and persevere, being not hearers
who forget but doers who act—they will be
blessed in their doing. (James 1:25)

I INVITE you to try a little experiment I have tried several times just to make a point about what typical believers think about their faith. (So far the experiment has never failed.) Ask a group of people to think about the word *sin* and to give some examples of sinful behavior. Typically, they will offer such responses as "lying," "stealing," or "cursing." A few might say "overeating." Those who are the least inhibited might mention impure sexual thoughts or behavior.

No matter the specifics, the point is that the responses are almost always negative. The truth is that most Christians instinctively think of sin as doing things we should not do rather than in terms of failing to do what we should do. Such an attitude owes more to contemporary Christian culture than to biblical teaching.

Those of us who are trying to become healthier fall victim to this same mentality when we take an entirely negative approach to losing weight. We exhibit this negative approach by focusing and dwelling on things we can't have, whether it be donuts, lasagna, potato chips, or cheesecake. A more positive approach would focus on what we *can* do. We can jog, lift weights, do sit-ups or crunches, go biking or hiking, or try a new sport.

We can choose to view the goal of becoming healthy as an exciting opportunity to engage life, to try something new. Or we can view it negatively, only in terms of self-denial, of depriving ourselves of things we enjoy. The irony is that the more we do positively to achieve the goal, the less we have to deny ourselves. Put another way, a brisk forty-minute walk around the park easily compensates for a donut or two.

Of course there are times to "just say no." But with so many positive options available, let's not forget how important and useful it can be to say yes!

❈   ❈   ❈

PRAYER: Dear God, may I recognize more fully this day that you are a positive God who created life and all that surrounds us to be experienced and enjoyed. May I say yes to the things of life at least as often as I say no.

God Said It Was ALL GOOD

God saw everything that he had made, and indeed, it was very good. And there was evening and there was morning, the sixth day. (Genesis 1:31)

TO do or say things that suggest that food is somehow "bad," we are, I believe, insulting God. We say eating carrot sticks or broccoli is good. But eating chocolate cake or Bavarian crème pie is bad. Sometimes after indulging we even say, "I've been bad."

In truth, eating food is not a morally neutral activity. Though it can be abused, it is essentially and overwhelmingly good. In addition to sustaining life, food has been given to us—in a variety of forms and smells, tastes and textures—for our enjoyment. That so many around the world do not enjoy the luxury of regarding food as anything more than a source of sustenance is a tragedy we all should be doing more to amend.

As with all other material resources and human experiences, food is meant to be enjoyed in appropriate ways and in cooperation with the laws of nature. Our starting point, however, must not be that food itself is somehow inherently evil or that eating certain foods is inherently wrong. Unfortunately, these kinds of messages have been getting through to too many of our daughters, some of whom are risking their health, and in some cases their lives, based on the mistaken belief, conscious or subconscious, that food lies at the source of their problems.

We cannot successfully lose weight or achieve optimum health if we begin by regarding food as the enemy. Far from being an enemy, food is in fact the source of our strength. It provides the vitamins and minerals and nutrients our bodies—our temples—require to accomplish our work, to experience the joys of life, and to praise and serve our Creator.

Success will come not from resisting food as we would resist an enemy, but from managing it. Food is our friend. And it is far easier to manage a friend than an enemy. When we appreciate the gift of food—even those sadly misnamed "decadent desserts"—we will not fall prey to unjustified, unhealthy, and counterproductive feelings of guilt. When we regard food as a gift instead of allowing it to hurt us, we will be in a better position to use it wisely as the good gift God intends.

✳ ✳ ✳

PRAYER: Thank you, Lord, for celery, broccoli, tomatoes, and zucchini. Thank you also for fruit pies and chocolate cake and barbecue potato chips. Thank you for all your good gifts. May we learn to manage them wisely.

Must a HABIT Always Be Bad?

Although Daniel knew that the document had
been signed, he continued to go to his house,
which had windows in its upper room open toward
Jerusalem, and to get down on this knees three
times a day to pray to his God and praise him,
just as he had done previously. (Daniel 6:10)

ALMOST every time I go on an out-of-town trip, I
can count on having forgotten something. On one particular business trip a few years ago, I left behind my
toothpaste and toothbrush. It didn't concern me much
when it occurred to me on the plane that I had forgotten them. I figured I could purchase these items at the
hotel gift shop.

Unfortunately, my flight was delayed, and by the time I
arrived, the gift shop was closed. I asked at the front desk
if there were any stores nearby. The man said he wasn't
sure if anything would be open so late at night, but he
pointed me toward two possibilities.

Feeling desperate, I ventured out into the night, only to find that everything was closed except for a few pizza places, which were not likely to have toothbrushes for sale. I returned to my room disappointed. I was fairly certain my teeth would not fall out just because I failed to brush on one night. Still, this was not good. I was in the habit of brushing my teeth at least two or three times a day and always before going to bed. I figured it had been at least thirty years since the last time I did not brush my teeth at bedtime.

The first thing next morning, I ran out to buy a new toothbrush and toothpaste, then hurried back to my room. It was the best tooth-brushing experience I've ever had. In fact, it was exhilarating. I savored the feel of the brush, the taste of the paste, the long-awaited feeling of freshness, for it had been tough to go even one night without giving in to my habit.

We are prone to think only of bad habits. For some, the words "bad" and "habit" are joined. But I realized through this experience that good habits can be just as hard to break as bad ones, whether it's saying "thank you" or brushing teeth.

Becoming healthy entails adopting and feeding healthy habits: drinking water after every meal, going to the produce section of the grocery store first, or walking or jogging. Once we cherish these habits and how they can help us, they'll become very hard to break. And we'll be better for it.

❈   ❈   ❈

PRAYER: Lord God, point me toward one new, positive activity I can begin today with the hope of turning it into a habit.

Choosing OBSESSIONS Wisely

Whatever your task, put yourselves into it,
as done for the Lord and not for your masters....
(Colossians 3:23)

NOT long ago, I underwent minor knee surgery. Prior to the surgery, a nurse marked the knee that was to be repaired. A few minutes later, the surgeon came in and was more than a little upset to discover that the knee had already been marked. "This isn't the way the system works," he bawled. "I'm the one who marks the knee. It's the way everyone knows I've talked with the patient."

"But each doctor has a different way of doing things," the nurse responded, trying to explain that it might well have been a very competent person who had committed the evil deed.

"That may be true," said the doctor. "But there's only one right way. And that's my way."

You get the idea. This doctor was obsessed with perfection, based on his own understanding of it. He was the kind of person I'd absolutely hate working for or serving on a church committee with. There's no way I'd want to live next door to him. Wouldn't think of having him over for dinner. But did I want him working on my knee? You bet I did!

I have a theory that all of us, or at least most of us, are obsessive about something. That is, we all have obsessive personalities when it comes to certain areas of our lives, even though we may be easygoing most of the time. And there are some obsessions (both good and bad) that we fade in and out of. For example, we have both eating binges and exercise binges.

Our ability to live successfully in some ways boils down to choosing our obsessions wisely. "Obsessive" need not be a negative word. A local grocery store chain is "fresh obsessed." That's a good thing. Most of us know people who are "obsessed" with running or with eating five servings of fruit or vegetables each day. These can be good things, too, although some people have unhealthy addictions to things otherwise good for us.

The point is that it's okay to be eccentric. In fact, some "all or nothing" type people have to be eccentric. Free your inner obsessive child! And may all your obsessions be positive ones.

❉   ❉   ❉

PRAYER: Dear God, some of your greatest servants throughout history have been eccentric, from John the Baptist to
Pope John Paul, from Martin Luther to Martin Luther King
Jr. May we be so eccentric, so focused, so obsessed about
doing what is right.

PUBLISHING Our Values

You yourselves are our letter, written on our hearts,
to be known and read by all…. (2 Corinthians 3:2)

ONE normally associates the word *war* with aggression.
Its opposite, *peace,* is commonly thought to be more of a
passive term. Thus, I was intrigued several years ago upon
encountering a bumper sticker with the two-word message "Wage Peace." I was drawn to the concept that peace
was something to create, not something to wait around
for. And so even though I'm not much of a bumper-sticker
person, I made an exception for "Wage Peace"—and
regretted it many times.

Until I bought that bumper sticker, I never realized
the extent to which I was vulnerable to road rage.
Many times I wanted to honk my horn or give someone
else an angry look because either they did something
stupid or I felt they were overreacting to something I
did that was stupid. But I felt powerless to respond
because I was a peace-wager. It said so right there on

my bumper. I was stuck. I had published my values for all the world to see. And now I had to live with them. I didn't mind being considered an angry driver, but I wanted at all costs to avoid the label of "hypocrite."

Now there are those who would say that my bumper sticker ultimately had a negative effect because it led me to repress my anger. But the other way to look at it is that it helped me to control my behavior. One could argue that, given the problems this country has with road rage, maybe we could use a healthy dose of repressed anger!

A positive approach to losing weight ought to include "publishing our values," making statements (mostly to ourselves), not about who we are, but about what we are striving to become. Notes on mirrors reminding us of our exercise goals. Perhaps a note on the refrigerator door nudging us to eat something green. Maybe even a friendly wager with a friend who is striving in a similar direction.

All these little things, just like that little, seemingly harmless bumper sticker, constitute a proactive way of keeping our goals and values visible, at the forefront of our lives.

❀ ❀ ❀

PRAYER: Lord God, help me to take a stand for my values and goals. Give me the courage to state them and the commitment to fulfill them.

VARIETY Is the Spice of Life

I know that there is nothing better
for them than to be happy and
enjoy themselves as long as they live;
moreover, it is God's gift that all should
eat and drink and take pleasure in all their toil.
(Ecclesiastes 3:12-13).

WE'VE all heard it said that some people eat to live while others live to eat. I'll always remember a former coworker I'll call John as one who truly modeled the notion of someone who lived to eat. The man had a huge potbelly and absolutely no shame. He was always first in line at company functions where food was served. John would go on a two-week vacation each year, often to interesting and exotic places. But upon returning, he would describe his vacation to smiling coworkers (who, like John, had no shame) almost exclusively in terms of the restaurants he had visited and the foods he had eaten.

Hopefully we all (including John) would agree that there is far more to life than eating. On the other hand, perhaps some of us ought to be a little more like John in our ability to recognize that good food is among the many gifts God has provided us.

Just as the devil doesn't have all the good music, neither does the devil have all the good food. I'm not the world's greatest gourmet cook, but I make a chicken scaloppini dish (made with white wine) that I've been told is four-star-restaurant quality. And it came from a healthy recipes cookbook! And have you ever tried a nice cut of salmon with nothing on it except some lemon juice and pepper?

Cutting back on foods we have for years been accustomed to eating—pizza with extra cheese and fast-food fries—does not have to be a wilderness experience. I enjoy many recipes that are as pleasing to the palate as they are healthy, and I'm convinced there are many, many more waiting to be discovered.

Nutritionists tell us that, beyond all the calories, variety in the diet is good. So instead of viewing adjusting our eating habits in terms of denying ourselves, we can view it as an opportunity to explore more of the gifts God has provided: new spices, new combinations, new colors, flavors, and textures. Like so many good things in life, they are out there just waiting to be discovered.

✳ ✳ ✳

PRAYER: Thank you, God, for all the healthy foods I have never tried and for spices whose names I can't pronounce. I commit today to expanding my dietary territory in ways that will make me healthier and more appreciative of all you have given us.

CLIMBING Every Mountain

✳ ✳ ✳ ✳ ✳ ✳ ✳ ✳ ✳ ✳ ✳ ✳ ✳ ✳ ✳ ✳ ✳

For everything created by God is good,
and nothing is to be rejected, provided it is
received with thanksgiving; for it is sanctified
by God's word and by prayer. (1 Timothy 4:4–5)

I RECENTLY heard a radio interview with a man in his early fifties who, his doctors told him, had less than a year to live. I was overcome by his sense of contentment, even joy, for the life he'd had. This man had absolutely no regrets for how he'd spent his days. Where there were mountains to climb, he climbed them; opportunities to seize, he seized them; sunsets to enjoy, he enjoyed them. Some people live life as if it is something to be endured. Others, like this man, view life as something to be savored.

I've heard it said somewhat euphemistically of overweight people that they have "too much appreciation" for the "finer things" in life. But I'm of the mind that the opposite is true. Perhaps we are overweight because we don't appreciate—don't savor—the finer things enough. We eat out of habit, by rote, in a hurry, without thinking. In short, we eat without appreciating, without savoring.

One of the reasons we eat too much is that we eat too fast. Nutritionists tell us that it takes several minutes for the stomach to get the message to the brain that it is content, full. When we eat by rote and in a hurry, we don't allow the time needed for nature as God designed it to take its course.

Without downgrading the role of mealtime prayers, I believe that the life of the Christian should be dominated by a constant sense of gratitude, of appreciation. When we eat, we ought to be aware of what we are eating, whether it's a fine steak or a peanut butter sandwich. We ought to be thankful, appreciative of every bite, and should show our appreciation by slowing down and enjoying the experience as God intended. Not only will slowing down help us in our effort to be content with less, but it will help keep us, in the words of a common prayer, "ever mindful of the needs of others," specifically those around the world who don't have the luxury of taking food for granted.

If we are unable to appreciate what we're eating—to be genuinely thankful—perhaps we should consider not eating it in the first place. Lack of appreciation might well be considered an indication that our eating is based not on hunger, but on habit.

It's no coincidence that *savory* is an adjective commonly used to define the finest foods. In truth, if we approach life with an attitude of gratefulness, we will savor everything we eat. And the more time we take to do so, the less food we will need to feel satisfied.

❋ ❋ ❋

PRAYER: Lord, help me to slow down. Increase my appreciation and sense of gratitude for life. May I learn and develop the art of savoring every bite.

doing YOUR part

You can't control outcomes.
You *can* control effort.

PROGRESS Takes Time

❈ ❈ ❈ ❈ ❈ ❈ ❈ ❈ ❈ ❈ ❈ ❈ ❈ ❈ ❈ ❈ ❈

And let us run with perseverance
the race that is set before us.... (Hebrews 12:1b)

WHEN I was in high school, if people made jokes about my physical appearance (and they did), it was because I was "too skinny." The summer before my senior year I had the opportunity to go to an outdoor sports camp. Because it was hot and the conditioning drills were fairly intense, the coaches made sure we took in plenty of water and that we weighed in twice a day.

I set a goal of gaining at least five pounds during my week away. At each meal I ate as much as I could, then shuffled off to the weight room to see if the scales would reward me. It didn't work. I couldn't even gain a pound.

Well, times have changed. I've accomplished my goal of gaining five pounds. In fact, I've far surpassed it! Now when I step on the scale, I think of feathers, puffy clouds, and cotton balls. But that doesn't work any better today than it did twenty-five years ago.

I've learned to hate my scale. Sometimes I feel like kicking it, and sometimes I act on that feeling. The truth is that the best thing I can do—and the best thing you can do—is to pack the scale away. Put it in a box and hide it in the attic for a month or four. After all, its *raison d'être*—its sole purpose for existence—is to discourage us with bad news as often as we allow it.

In this culture of instant gratification, many have learned to expect instant rewards. We have lost sight of the concept of patience as a virtue. We want results, and we want them now. We didn't gain thirty unwanted pounds in a day, but often it seems we expect to lose it in one. Some dieters weigh themselves three, four, five times a day, and if the result is not what they were expecting (and it almost never is), they feel discouraged, disappointed, ready to give up the fight.

Hebrews 12:1-8 reminds us that life as a follower of Christ is not a 100-yard dash; it's a marathon. Whether the goal is losing weight or growing toward spiritual maturity, progress takes time, patience, hard work, and perseverance.

So pack the scale away, at least for a few weeks. Don't worry so much about how you're doing. Concentrate instead on *what* you are doing from day to day. The weeks and months will find a way of taking care of themselves. Hopefully, so will the pounds.

※　※　※

PRAYER: Dear God, are you sometimes disappointed that your followers are so demanding? We want results without commitment, rewards without sacrifice. Teach us to be patient. Give us strength to persevere, to press on even when our efforts seem useless. Teach us to wait, and be with us in the waiting. Amen.

STRENGTH for Today

The steadfast love of the LORD never ceases,
   his mercies never come to an end;
      they are new every morning;
   great is your faithfulness.
—Lamentations 3:22–23

I ONCE read an interview with a celebrity—a man in his thirties—who, like countless others, each day waged war with alcoholism. As he described the nature of his struggle, it struck me that in his life alcohol had taken on some of the characteristics of a lover. For example, as he would a lover, he thought about alcohol many times each day. He longed for it to fulfill a deep desire. It was a source of comfort in his life; his choice to live without it was not an easy one. But despite these feelings, he knew that it was best for him and for all who cared about him—that this love—this passion—go unrequited.

This man admitted that he could not face the prospect of going the rest of his life without ever taking another drink. The thought of it was too overwhelming. In fact, it was virtually inconceivable to him. But while he could not imagine going an entire lifetime, he *could* imagine going another day. In this way—by breaking life down into smaller chunks—he was able to manage his problem.

When the whole of life seems unmanageable or too threatening because of the magnitude of the problems and challenges we face, we too can respond by focusing on the day at hand. Or if the day seems unmanageable, we can focus on the hour or minutes at hand and simply determine to do the best we can, for that is all we can do.

We can focus on the smaller picture, on doing our part, because of the faith we have that the bigger picture is in God's hands. Perhaps the strength we feel we lack for the long run will arrive when we need it, day by day.

In some ways, the decision to become healthier must be a choice we make for life, for it entails making permanent lifestyle changes. As with the man who struggles with alcohol, we may find it impossible to imagine sustaining these changes for a year, or ten years, or fifty. Allow God to worry about the bigger picture. If you have strength for today, use it. And do the same tomorrow.

❋　❋　❋

PRAYER: Heavenly Lord, I know that my future is safe in your hands. May I find in this knowledge the freedom to address to the best of my ability the concerns of today.

The Importance of a GOOD PLAN

Where there is no prophecy,
    the people cast off restraint,
  but happy are those who keep the law.
            —Proverbs 29:18

NOT long ago I accompanied our church youth group on a whitewater rafting adventure. It was my first time. As one who is not overly amphibious, I determined that my main goal was to stay above water. I was not the only "rookie" aboard with this goal in mind. Thus, our group paid especially close attention to our guide's instructions.

At first the river was slow, so we had plenty of time to learn the basic rafting vocabulary and to practice working together before the waters got rougher. For each situation we might encounter, we had not only a plan, but a back-up plan. Our guide alerted us that he might instruct us to do something against what our natural instincts might be, adding that our best chance of making it safely to our destination was to follow his instructions.

The whole experience ended up being a good "object lesson" for our young people. I talked with several of them later about how important it is to think in advance about the rough waters ahead in their lives and to have a good plan in place to deal with those waters. I told them,

"To be in a situation where someone is pressuring you to do something you feel uncomfortable doing is no time to be thinking about what is right and what is wrong or about what your plan should be."

This same principle applies to our efforts to lose weight and become healthier. If we wait till the alarm goes off at 6:00 a.m. to decide whether or not to go jogging, chances are we won't go. Similarly, if we wait till 10:00 p.m. to consider whether a slice of chocolate cake fits into our weight-loss plans, the answer is almost sure to be yes.

It's important—vital—to have a plan in place, to have commitments that will sustain us in the heat of the battles we will face. This does not mean that we will be able to win every battle, but it greatly increases the odds.

❊ ❊ ❊

PRAYER: From the beginning of time, O God, you had a plan. Help me to appreciate the value of a good plan for my life, a plan that enables me to respond appropriately and intelligently in the heat of the battle and to accomplish the goals I have set.

An Issue of PRIORITIES

His master said to him, "Well done, good and trustworthy slave; you have been trustworthy in a few things, I will put you in charge of many things; enter into the joy of your master." (Matthew 25:21)

RECENTLY, I was with a group of people among whom the topic of reading habits and preferences came up. Someone posed the question, "How many think you could read thirty books a year if you really tried?" Only one or two avid readers were convinced they could accomplish such a feat. (For some of those in attendance, reading three or four books in a year's time would be a big accomplishment.)

"Thirty is a lot," the man acknowledged. "But how many of you think you could read, say, twenty pages a day?" This time, except for a few nonreaders, every hand was raised. The trap had been set, and pretty much everyone fell into it. You see, assuming an average book length of two hundred pages, reading twenty pages a day would yield a result of over thirty-six books in the course of a year!

Sometimes the ability to achieve our goals is influenced by the way we formulate them. Many people consider it unrealistic to find the time to exercise for at least thirty minutes five times a week. Perhaps it helps to put this amount of time in perspective by looking at how much time the typical person spends on other activities: sleeping (forty-nine hours a week), eating (seven hours a week), watching mindless television (about fifteen hours a week, but for some a lot more).

If we exercised for just one-tenth of the time we spend eating, sleeping, and watching TV, we would be exercising for over an hour each day. Thus, at some point, we must honestly ask ourselves if an unwillingness to exercise is truly an issue of time or of priorities, especially when it is possible to combine activities, for example, by riding an exercise bike while watching mindless television.

No one need own elaborate exercise equipment or belong to a health club to get the exercise he or she needs. Moving around a few dumbbells, a walk through the neighborhood, and sit-ups and push-ups are within most persons' easy reach.

Christian living, by and large, is about choosing priorities at many levels: Is it more important to earn more money or to spend time with my family? Will I spend part of my vacation time on a missions trip, or will I spend it all on myself? Will I create space in my busy (or perhaps my not-so-busy) schedule for exercise? That's what it will take if you accept the challenge to do your part.

❋　❋　❋

PRAYER: Lord, I confess that my priorities are sometimes out of alignment. Make me more conscious of how I spend my time and energy. Help me to realign my priorities as part of an effort to do my part.

The Kids Are Right: IT ISN'T FAIR

❋ ❋ ❋ ❋ ❋ ❋ ❋ ❋ ❋ ❋ ❋ ❋ ❋ ❋ ❋ ❋ ❋

But Martha was distracted by her many tasks;
so she came to him and asked,
"Lord, do you not care that my sister
has left me to do all the work by myself?
Tell her then to help me." (Luke 10:40)

MY father-in-law, now in his late sixties, is six feet tall. Though he has always stayed active fixing things and doing home improvement projects, for the more than twenty years I've known him, he has never exercised beyond an occasional walk. He has a healthy appetite—loves prime rib, won't eat "rabbit food," and is never shy about ordering dessert.

As far as I am concerned, my father-in-law deserves to weigh about 270 pounds. Instead, he weighs less than 170, over 100 pounds less than I think he deserves to weigh. I, on the other hand, have exercised regularly for virtually my whole life. And though I admit I eat more than I should, I often don't eat nearly as much as I could.

The reward I get is to be 30 pounds over what most doctors would recommend. It's not fair.

Studies have shown that, statistically, the offspring of two overweight parents have little chance (about one in five) of avoiding having a weight problem themselves. Some blame inherited genes, while others point to inherited environment—that is, a home in which high-calorie foods were encouraged more enthusiastically than high-intensity physical activity. Most likely it's a combination of the two.

Whatever the case, I stand by my conviction that life is not fair. I've thought about inventing a scale in which you would input information about the food you've eaten and the exercise you've done. And when you step on it, it would tell you how much you deserve to weigh instead of how much you actually weigh. But such a scale wouldn't solve my problem—or yours.

The story of Mary and Martha is one of many accounts in the Bible that suggest to us that life, from our perspective, does not always seem fair. In fact, God never said it would be. We can whine about it and allow it to crush our will and keep us from trying, or we can accept it and consider that things could be worse. It may not be possible for some of us ever to weigh what we would like to weigh, but we can choose to be overweight and healthy or overweight and unhealthy. In terms of reaching that "ideal weight," we may not be able to do enough. But we are able to do something. We are able to do the best we can.

❊ ❊ ❊

PRAYER: Dear God, grant me the grace to understand the need to focus on doing my part and on doing my best and to allow you to worry about what is "fair."

STARTING Small

We, however, will not boast beyond limits, but will
keep within the field that God has assigned to us,
to reach out even as far as you. (2 Corinthians 10:13)

AT a party during the Christmas season, the topic of
New Year's resolutions came up. A man proudly
announced that so far he had kept all his resolutions
for the current year, which was quite impressive con-
sidering he had only a few days left to go. Naturally,
people asked him what resolutions he'd made those
many months ago. His response went something like
this: "Not to gain more than thirty pounds this year;
not to go more than sixty miles an hour in a thirty-five-
mile-per-hour zone; and to read at least one book."
Needless to say, glad as people were that he'd kept his
resolutions, no one was in a hurry to get in line and
shake his hand.

I will not uphold this man as the model New Year's res-
olution maker, but there is something to be learned from

his approach: His resolutions were attainable. A little too attainable, to be sure, but at least they were attainable. Our tendency is to err in the other direction. We make resolutions that don't take into account our personal limitations or the reality of our life's circumstances. As a result, we can't even last a week, let alone make it to Groundhog Day. Feeling like failures, we quit trying. (Go to any YMCA or health club, and they'll tell you that their busiest time of year is the first two weeks of January!)

Our challenge is to find the right balance between stretching our limitations and denying them, between improving ourselves and expecting that we become someone we're not. This means making commitments to change that lie somewhere between resolving not to be convicted of a felony and winning the Boston Marathon. For example, resolving not to eat anything rich in fat after 7:00 P.M. should be doable. (High-calorie foods consumed later in the day are more likely to be stored as fat.) Walking for thirty minutes three times a week is a little under what is recommended, but it's a great start and it's far better than doing nothing.

❋ ❋ ❋

PRAYER: Lord, help me to be content in starting small. Guide me in the process of selecting simple, attainable, but meaningful goals, goals that stretch me without pulling me apart.

PATIENCE Is a Virtue

※ ※ ※ ※ ※ ※ ※ ※ ※ ※ ※ ※ ※ ※ ※ ※ ※

Be patient, therefore, beloved, until the coming
of the Lord. The farmer waits for the precious crop
from the earth, being patient with it until it receives
the early and the late rains. You also must be patient.
(James 5:7–8a)

ARGUABLY, the most telling image of our time is
the image of someone pacing in front of the
microwave. Food that once took hours to cook can
now be cooked in minutes. The minutes once required
to reheat food have been reduced to seconds. But for
most of us, that's still not fast enough.

A worldwide industry worth countless billions of dollars
has evolved over the last three decades or so, not around bet-
ter-tasting or more nutritious food, but around faster food.

There was a time not long ago when a 286 (processing
speed) computer was faster than anyone had ever desired.

But today, the 286 is considered a dinosaur. "Fast" gave way to "faster," which in turn gave way to "faster still." Nowadays any speed short of being virtually instantaneous is considered unacceptable and inefficient.

Enter the television advertisement or infomercial: "Lose thirty pounds in thirty days." Those making money off these schemes know that "Lose ten pounds in six months!" or "Maintain your current weight for two years!" are not very marketable come-ons. But the plain truth is that no knowledgeable person who cares about you—and not just about getting your money—would ever encourage you to lose thirty pounds in thirty days. According to conventional medical wisdom, it is neither safe (in terms of our health) nor smart (with regard to permanent weight loss) to lose more than one or two pounds a week.

Losing weight faster than that (especially if it is accomplished by not eating) is almost certain to slow down the body's metabolism, making it far more difficult in the long run to maintain the lower body weight and far easier to gain it back and even put on additional pounds.

The goal of losing weight can be likened to a life of faith. It revolves not around doing what seems to work best for the moment, but around making commitments to principles and ideals that can carry us for the long haul. In short, it means doing what is right instead of what works the quickest.

The Chinese bamboo tree is an appropriate illustration. It does nothing for the first four years except grow its root system underground. Then, in year five, it grows from a height of nothing to eighty feet. Plant your seeds. Grow your roots. When your results come, they will last.

❋   ❋   ❋

PRAYER: Grant me, O Lord, the comfort that comes from knowing I am trying to do what is right. And then the patience to await and the ability to accept whatever results your grace provides.

The VICTORY Is in the Struggle

❋ ❋ ❋ ❋ ❋ ❋ ❋ ❋ ❋ ❋ ❋ ❋ ❋ ❋ ❋ ❋ ❋

So let us not grow weary in doing what is right,
for we will reap at harvest time, if we do not give up.
(Galatians 6:9)

A CERTAIN line of work now stands at or near the top of many a person's "Most Despicable Professions" list. I'm thinking not of the usual suspects—lawyers, politicians, and used-car salespersons—but of the ubiquitous telemarketer, who enters our homes uninvited every night around 6:00.

I confess to having a soft spot in my heart for telemarketers. The person on the other end of the line is, after all, a person. I consider the possibility that he or she must be desperate for a job and must hate being a telemarketer more than we hate getting called by them.

And at some level I admire telemarketers. In fact, I admire anyone who gets hung up on, dismissed, insulted, ignored, yelled at, and demeaned, but keeps right on trying. I once heard a presentation on what it takes to become a successful salesperson. The speaker offered case studies of two salespersons, one who succeeded and the other who failed. The two had the same resources for getting started. They had the same background and experience. Their sales territories and opportunities were comparable. The only difference was that one was defeated by failure and disappointment, while the other pressed on in the midst of it.

The goal of becoming healthier and happier is a goal for a lifetime. We will experience victories in this struggle but also times of failure, times when we feel we did not live up to our commitments, when we feel as if we let others or ourselves down. The same is true with our lives in general. The only question is whether we will allow disappointment, defeats, and frustrations to have the final say.

We must learn to regard defeat not as the end of things, but as a normal part of life, and perhaps even as an opportunity to lick our wounds and start again. Similarly, we must learn to view victory, not only in terms of living up to society's expectations or even to our own goals, but rather in terms of persisting in the struggle, not giving up.

We worship a God who expects a lot only from those who have been given a lot to work with. Some of us have greater odds to conquer than others. Remember you are loved. Be encouraged to follow what is right and to do the best you can. And don't hesitate to call it "victory."

❋ ❋ ❋

PRAYER: Dear God, I recognize that the path you have called me to walk is not always easy. Sometimes I will falter. Sometimes I will fall. When I do, give me the strength not to give up. Grant me the courage to get back up and try again, realizing that the victory is not in the results, but in the struggle.

In CONCLUSION ...

ANY author wants to change her or his readers in some way. My hope is that something you have read in these pages or encountered in Scripture has made a difference. Perhaps you've learned something new about how to define and achieve success in losing weight and becoming healthier. More important, perhaps you have gained some new perspectives and, along with them, a needed boost of inspiration and motivation. As you contemplate continuing on the journey you have begun—or as you start anew—I hope that the following principles, perspectives, and prescriptions will continue to guide you on your path.

1. God loves you and accepts you unconditionally as you are, no matter how much you weigh, what you look like, or what you may think of yourself, and no matter how many times you feel you've tried and failed.

2. Your body is a gift from God, a temple of the Holy Spirit. Taking good care of it is an opportunity to say thank you.

3. Tend to your spirit. You are not a merely physical being. The health of your spirit will go a long way toward determining the health of your body.

4. Eat when you are hungry. Both food and cravings for food are gifts from God.

5. Try to uncover and address the reasons you eat when you are not hungry. Remember that food can meet physical needs but not emotional ones.

6. Ask for help when you need it, and be there to support others. Walk with your friends, both figuratively and literally!

7. Remember the words of the Chinese philosopher who said, "The journey of a thousand miles begins with a single step."

8. Focus on obedience—on doing your part, on doing the best you can. Find freedom with the realization that the results are not fully within your control. Define success in terms of the striving.

9. Approach your goals proactively, positively. Instead of thinking about what you can't eat or do, focus on what you can do. Become a gourmet cook of healthy foods. Go hiking and biking. Explore, run, play. Take up a new hobby. Drink lots of water. Breathe in the fresh air. Listen to the birds at sunrise. In a word, live!

10. You can do this! Others have, and you can, too. God bless you on your journey.